SOUTHERN KETO BEYOND BASICS

40+ Mouth-Watering and Easy-To-Cook Southern Based Keto Recipes, Thatare Low Carb and High Fat For Busy People in This Practical Approach of Fat Burn and Health Improvement

Table of Contents

INTRODUCTION

A ketogenic diet is made chiefly out of calories from fat and just few calories from starches. The diet powers the body to devour fat rather than carbs for energy. When in doubt, the starches you eat are changed over into glucose in the body, used to the energy around the body and in the mind. In any case, in the event that you neglected to eat enough sugars, your body will utilize a crisis framework to consume fat. The EU can eat the put away fat and fat you eat for energy. The put away fat is separated into two sections, the fattest acids, and the ketone bodies. The Ceton bodies bring the cerebrum's energy rather than glucose. This state of numerous ketone bodies in your blood is called ketosis.

The ketogenic way of life doesn't need a penance of flavor! Numerous individuals feel that going Keto implies they need to surrender American conventional dishes; however with a little imagination the vast majority of your number one food varieties can be made Keto. Southern Keto will tell you the best way to make your number one solace food sources delightful and low-carb. You don't need to quit any pretense of breading, cheesecake, seared chicken, or rolls.

Keto southern meals

30+ recipes

1. Southern crockpot chicken taco soup (easy Keto dinner recipe)

Cook Time: 56 min Total Time: 1 Hour + 10 Min | Yield: 8

Ingredients:

- 2 Pounds Chicken Breasts (Or Thighs – Use What You've Got)
- 4 Cups Chicken Broth
- 2 10 Ounce Cans Rotel Tomatoes
- 2 8 Ounce Packs Cream Cheese
- 4 Cloves Minced Garlic
- ½ Cup Onion (Diced)
- Tablespoons Cumin

- 1 Teaspoon Chili Powder
- 1 Teaspoon Paprika
- ¼ Teaspoon Salt
- 3 Tablespoons Lemon Juice
- ½ Tablespoon Lime Juice
- Discretionary Toppings
- Cheddar Cheese
- Green Onions
- Cut Jalapenos
- Diced Tomatoes
- Acrid Cream

Directions

1. In case you're searching for 1,000,000 stages and a huge load of data about how to prepare a slow cooker formula, at that point you're stuck between a rock and a hard place here. This one is a toss and go.
2. Spot your defrosted chicken in the stewing pot.
3. Add the onions. Or on the other hand skirt the onions in the event that you like to make this soup without a couple of extra carbs or in case you're recently out of onions.
4. Top the chicken with the garlic, cumin, bean stew powder, paprika, salt, lemon, and lime juice.
5. At that point add the chicken stock – and the tomatoes – and set the simmering pot on high and accomplish something fantastic with the following four hours of your life.

6. After you've hot the four-hour mark, shred the chicken – add the cream cheddar and mix. Supper is served.

Notes

7. In case you're freezing this soup, leave out the cream cheddar.
8. You can add it in after you defrost. Store in an impermeable compartment– with a mark, so it doesn't get lost, and freeze for as long as 3 months.
9. Serves 8

Nutritional value:

- Calories Per Serving: 360

% DAILY VALUE

- 30%Total Fat 23.1g
- Saturated Fat 12.2g
- Trans Fat 0g
- Polyunsaturated Fat 1.5g
- 0%Monounsaturated Fat 5.9g
- 34%Sodium 780.8mg
- 3%Total Carbohydrate 7.5g
- 5%Dietary Fiber 1.5g
- Sugars 4.6g
- 61%Protein 30.6g
- 23%Vitamin A 210.6μg
- 11%Vitamin C 10mg

2. Southern Cabbage Soup with Meatballs

Prep time: 5 min |Cook time: 25 min |Serving 2-4

Ingredients
Soup base

- 2 large slices ginger
- 3 to 4 green onions , chopped
- (Option 1) Quick pork and chicken broth
- 1/4 cup chopped pancetta (or bacon)
- 1 cup chicken stock (or 2 cups, if you want the soup to be extra rich) (Optional)
- (Option 2) Clear seafood broth
- 1/4 cup dried shrimp
- 1/4 cup dried scallops
- (Option 3) Easy broth
- 3 cups chicken stock (or pork stock)

Meatballs

- 1/2 pound (230 grams) ground turkey (or ground pork)
- 1/4 cup finely chopped green onion (green part) (Optional)
- 1 tablespoon Shaoxing wine (or dry sherry or Japanese sake)
- 2 teaspoons or tamari for gluten-free
- 2 teaspoons potato starch
- 1 teaspoon ginger , grated
- 1 large egg
- 1/4 teaspoon salt
- 1 teaspoon sesame oil (or peanut oil, or vegetable oil)

Soup base

- 2 enormous cuts ginger
- 3 to 4 green onions , chopped
- (Alternative 1) Quick pork and chicken stock
- 1/4 cup chopped pancetta (or bacon)
- 1 cup chicken stock (or 2 cups, in the event that you need the soup to be additional rich) (Optional)
- (Alternative 2) Clear fish stock
- 1/4 cup dried shrimp
- 1/4 cup dried scallops
- (Alternative 3) Easy stock
- 3 cups chicken stock (or pork stock)

Meatballs

- 1/2 pound (230 grams) ground turkey (or ground pork)
- 1/4 cup finely chopped green onion (green part) (Optional)
- 1 tablespoon Shaoxing wine (or dry sherry or Japanese purpose)
- 2 teaspoons or tamari for sans gluten
- 2 teaspoons potato starch
- 1 teaspoon ginger , ground
- 1 huge egg
- 1/4 teaspoon salt
- 1 teaspoon sesame oil (or nut oil, or vegetable oil)
- Soup
- 6 to 8 huge napa cabbage leaves , chopped (create 6 to 8 cups)
- 1/2 daikon radish, stripped and chopped (creates 2 cups) (Optional)
- 1 clump enoki mushrooms brilliant needle mushrooms, intense closures eliminated and isolated
- 1/2 (400g/14-ounces) block delicate tofu , chopped
- Ocean salt to taste

Directions

1. Soup base alternative 1 - Quick pork and chicken stock
2. Heat a 3.8-liter (4-quart) pot over medium heat and add the greasy pieces of the pancetta. At the point when it begins to sizzle, go to medium low heat. Blending once in a while, cook until the fat renders and the pancetta becomes brilliant.
3. Add the lean pieces of the pancetta. Keep cooking and blending until brown.
4. Add chicken stock and promptly utilize a spatula to scratch the brown pieces off the lower part of the pot. Add 2 cups water (add 1 cup water, if using 2 cups chicken stock; or 3 cups water + 1 tablespoon shellfish sauce or hoisin sauce, in the event that you would prefer not to utilize chicken stock), ginger, and green onion. Cook over high heat until bubbling. Go to medium low heat. Cover and bubble for 5 minutes.
5. Soup base choice 2 - Clear fish stock
6. Flush dried scallops. Spot scallops in a little bowl and add water to cover. Rehydrate for 2 to 3 hours. Channel and attack little pieces.
7. Wash dried shrimp, move to a little bowl, and add water to cover. Rehydrate for 30 minutes. Channel and put in a safe spot.
8. Join the rehydrated scallops and shrimp, ginger, green onion, and 3 cups water in a 3.8-liter (4-quart) pot. Heat over high heat until bubbling. Go to medium heat. Cover and let stew for 5 minutes.

9. Soup base alternative 3 - Easy stock
10. Join chicken stock (or pork stock), ginger, and green onion in a 3.8-liter (4-quart) pot. Heat over high heat until bubbling. Go to medium heat. Cover and bubble for 5 minutes.

Meatballs

1. Consolidate every one of the ingredients for the meatballs in an enormous bowl. Mix until all ingredients are simply joined and structure a somewhat runny blend. Don't over-mix it. Let sit for 5 to 10 minutes.

Soup

1. Wash and cut veggies while letting the stock stew.
2. Add daikon radish into the soup pot. Cover and cook for 5 minutes.
3. Add the thick pieces of the napa cabbage. Cover and cook for 5 minutes.
4. Add the green pieces of the napa cabbage and enoki mushroom into the soup. Cook for 2 to 3 minutes.
5. You can change the flavoring now, by adding somewhat salt, if necessary.
6. Add delicate tofu. Push every one of the ingredients aside of the pot, to clear some space for the meatballs. (On the off chance that you need more space in the pot, you can take out a portion of the napa cabbage leaves)
7. Utilize a spoon to scoop 1 to 1.5 tablespoons of the meatball blend and cautiously add it into

the soup. Rehash this until you've made around 15 meatballs.

8. Cover the pot and stew until the meatballs are simply cooked through, 4 to 5 minutes. Mood killer heat promptly and eliminate the pot from the oven, keeping it covered.
9. Serve hot as a principle or side. To make it a full dinner, you can heat up certain noodles (or mung bean noodles or shirataki noodles) and add them into the soup toward the finish of cooking. For this situation, you should add a smidgen more salt or light soy sauce, to make the stock somewhat saltier. Thusly, it will taste perfectly with the noodles.

Nutrition

- Serving: 479g
- Calories: 222kcal
- Carbohydrates: 11.7g
- Protein: 23.6g
- Fat: 11g
- Saturated Fat: 2g
- Cholesterol: 104mg
- Sodium: 1078mg
- Potassium: 695mg
- Fiber: 2g
- Sugar: 4.2g
- Vitamin A: 6400IU
- Vitamin C: 89.1mg
- Calcium: 230mg
- Iron: 4mg

3. New Orleans BBQ Shrimp (Keto, Low-Carb)

Prep Time10 minutes |Cook Time10 minutes |Total Time20 minutes |Servings4 servings

Ingredients

- 1 pound shrimp stripped and deveined
- 1 tbsp. Worcestershire sauce
- 3 tsp. Cajun preparing
- 2 cloves garlic minced finely
- 1 tsp. lemon juice
- 4 tbsp. unsalted margarine
- 1 tbsp. water
- 2 tbsp. green onions chopped

Guidelines

1. Strip and devein the shrimp, clean them and put them in a safe spot.
2. Heat an enormous skillet over medium heat and soften the margarine. Add the garlic and Cajun preparing and cook for 1 moment. Add the shrimp, and throw until cooked. Around 3-4 minutes relying upon the size of your shrimp.
3. Mood killer the heat. Add the Worcestershire sauce to the skillet, the lemon juice, and the water to make somewhat of a sauce. Check for preparing, adding more salt if vital.
4. Embellishment with chopped green onions and serve!

Nutrition

- Serving: 0.25of the total
- Calories: 226kcal
- Carbohydrates: 3g
- Protein: 24g
- Fat: 13g
- Saturated Fat: 7g
- Cholesterol: 316mg
- Sodium: 926mg
- Potassium: 164mg
- Fiber: 1g
- Sugar: 1g
- Vitamin A: 1229IU
- Vitamin C: 8mg
- Calcium: 179mg
- Iron: 3mg
- Net Carbohydrates: 2g

4. Easy Southern Salmon Cakes

Total: 45 mins |Servings: 4x8(2 cakes per dish)

Ingredients

- 3 teaspoons extra-virgin olive oil, partitioned
- 1 little onion, finely chopped
- 1 stem celery, finely diced
- 2 tablespoons chopped new parsley
- 15 ounces canned salmon, depleted, or 1/2 cups cooked salmon
- 1 enormous egg, softly beaten
- 1 ½ teaspoons Dijon mustard
- 1 3/4 cups new entire wheat breadcrumbs,
- ½ teaspoon newly ground pepper
- Rich Dill Sauce, (formula follows)
- 1 lemon, cut into wedges

Directions:

Stage 1

1. Preheat oven to 450 degrees F. Coat a preparing sheet with cooking shower.

Stage 2

2. Heat 1/2 teaspoons oil in an enormous nonstick skillet over medium-high heat. Add onion and celery; cook, blending, until mellowed, around 3 minutes. Mix in parsley; eliminate from the heat.

Stage 3

3. Spot salmon in a medium bowl. Piece separated with a fork; eliminate any bones and skin. Add egg and mustard; blend well. Add the onion combination, breadcrumbs and pepper; blend well. Shape the blend into 8 patties, around 2 1/2 inches wide.

Stage 4

4. Heat remaining ½ teaspoons oil in the pan over medium heat. Add 4 patties and cook until the undersides are brilliant, 2 to 3 minutes. Using a wide spatula, turn them over onto the readied heating sheet. Rehash with the remaining patties.

Stage 5

5. Prepare the salmon cakes until brilliant on top and heated through, 15 to 20 minutes. In the

interim, get ready Creamy Dill Sauce. Serve salmon cakes with sauce and lemon wedges.

Nutrition Facts

- Per Serving:
- 350 calories
- Protein 34.4g
- Carbohydrates 25.8g
- Dietary fiber 5.7g
- Sugars 5.5g
- Fat 13.7g
- saturated fat 1.4g
- Cholesterol 126.3mg
- Vitamin a iu 418.7IU
- Vitamin c 7.4mg
- Folate 26.4mcg
- Calcium 60.3mg
- Iron 2.2mg
- Magnesium 58.9mg
- Potassium 168.7mg
- Sodium 761.4mg
- Thiamin 0.2mg.
- Exchanges:
- 1 1/2 Starch
- 1/2 Vegetable
- 3 1/2 Lean Protein
- 1 Fat

5. Keto Gumbo Recipe

Cook Time 1 hour |Total Time 1 hour |Servings:8

Ingredients:

- 12 oz. Andouille wiener (cut meagerly)
- 2 huge Bell peppers (diced; I utilized red and green)
- 1/2 huge Onion (diced)
- 1/2 cup Celery (diced)
- 4 cloves Garlic (minced)
- 8 cups Chicken stock
- 1 14.5-oz can Diced tomatoes (with fluid)
- 2 tbsp. Cajun preparing (start with 1 tbsp. on the off chance that you don't need zesty)
- 1/2 tsp. Sea salt (to taste)
- 24 oz. Cauliflower rice (new or frozen)
- 12 oz. Medium shrimp (stripped and deveined, defrosted whenever frozen)
- 1-3 tsp. File powder

Guidelines:

1. In a little skillet over medium heat, cook the okra for around 5 minutes, until any ooze cooks away.
2. Heat the oil in an enormous Dutch oven over medium heat. Add the ringer peppers, onions, and celery. Sauté for 5-8 minutes, until the vegetables are delicate.
3. Add the cut wiener. Sauté for around 5 minutes, until browned.
4. Make a well in the middle and add the minced garlic. Allow it to sizzle for around 30 seconds, until fragrant; at that point mix in with all the other things.
5. Add the chicken stock, diced tomatoes, and sautéed okra. Season with Cajun preparing and ocean salt to taste.
6. Heat the gumbo to the point of boiling, at that point cover and stew for 30 minutes.
7. Add the shrimp. Stew for 5 minutes.
8. Add the cauliflower rice. Stew for 5 minutes once more, until shrimp is murky and cauliflower rice is delicate.
9. Eliminate from heat. Sprinkle gumbo with record powder and mix, until thickened.

Nutrition Facts

- Amount per serving. Serving size in recipe notes above.
- Calories242
- Fat13.9g
- Protein17g
- Total Carbs12.8g
- Net Carbs8.6g
- Fiber4.2g
- Sugar4.8g

6. Tomato Noodle Soup

Prep Time: 5 Minutes | Cook Time: 20 Minutes | Total Time: 25 Minutes | Servings: 4

Ingredients

- 1 tablespoon vegetable oil
- 2 tablespoons green onion , chopped
- 3 tomatoes , chopped (or 2 16-ounce jars tomato)
- 8 cups pork stock (or chicken stock or water)
- 200 grams (7 ounces) udon noodles , dried (or frozen wontons)
- 8 braised pork ribs (or hamburger or chicken stew extra with sauce)
- salt , to taste
- 4 eggs (Optional)
- 2 cups infant bok choy , for design (Optional)

Guidelines

1. Heat a pot of water to the point of boiling to cook the noodles.
2. Heat oil in an enormous skillet over medium high heat until warm. Add green onion and mix a couple of times until fragrant. Add tomato and mix and slash until it nearly turns into a paste, 3 to 5 minutes.
3. Move the tomato paste to an enormous pot. Add pork stock (or chicken stock or water) and heat to the point of boiling over medium high heat. Go to low heat, cover, and let stew.
4. While stewing the stock, cook the noodles as indicated by the guidelines.
5. Five minutes before noodles are done, add pork ribs (or whatever extra meat you're using) and a spoonful of sauce to the noodle soup. Mix a couple of times until the sauce is blended well in with the stock. Taste the stock and add more salt if important. The stock should taste marginally pungent without anyone else. Add eggs. Cover and stew for another 2 to 3 minutes, until the eggs are half cooked (or more on the off chance that you like them to be completely cooked).
6. Channel the noodles and split them between 3 enormous dishes. Top the noodles with bok choy (discretionary). Pour the tomato stock over the bok choy with the goal that the hot stock rapidly cooks it (be mindful so as not to break the egg yolks!). Move an egg several pork ribs to each bowl.
7. Serve right away.

Nutrition

- Serving: 739g
- Calories: 423kcal
- Carbohydrates: 40.6g
- Protein: 27.7g
- Fat: 17.7g
- Saturated Fat: 5.1g
- Cholesterol: 194mg
- Sodium: 2005mg
- Potassium: 529mg
- Fiber: 4.3g
- Sugar: 7.8g
- Vitamin A: 2600IU
- Vitamin C: 39.6mg
- Calcium: 70mg
- Iron: 3.1mg

7. Keto southern Meaty Arugula Pizza

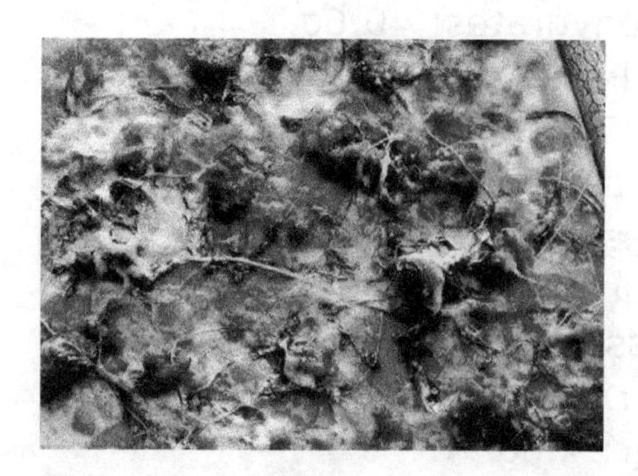

Total Time: 50 min |Prep: 40 min + rising | Bake: 10 min |Makes2 pizzas (8 pieces each)

Ingredients

- 1 bundle (1/4 ounce) dynamic dry yeast
- 1-1/2 cups warm water (110° to 115°)
- 2 tablespoons olive oil
- 2 teaspoons salt
- 1 teaspoon sugar
- 3-1/2 to 4 cups bread flour
- 4 teaspoons cornmeal

Fixings:

- 1 pound mass Italian wiener
- 2 tablespoons olive oil
- 6 garlic cloves, minced
- 1-1/2 cups shredded part-skim mozzarella cheddar
- 1 bundle (3-1/2 ounces) cut pepperoni
- 4 cups new arugula or child spinach
- 1/2 cup ground Parmesan cheddar

- Extra new arugula or child spinach, optional

Directions

1. In a small bowl, break up yeast in warm water. In a huge bowl, join 2 tablespoons oil, salt, sugar, yeast combination and 1-1/2 cups flour; beat on medium speed 3 minutes until smooth. Mix in sufficient excess flour to shape a delicate batter (mixture will be tacky).
2. Turn batter onto a floured surface; work until smooth and versatile, around 6-8 minutes. Spot in a lubed bowl, going once to oil the top. Cover with saran wrap and let ascend in a warm spot until multiplied, around 1-1/2 hours.
3. Preheat oven to 425°. Oil two 15x10x1-in. heating container; sprinkle with cornmeal. Punch down batter. Turn onto a daintily floured surface; partition fifty-fifty. Fold each into a 15x10-in. square shape; move to arranged container, squeezing edges to frame an edge. Cover with saran wrap; let rest 10 minutes.
4. In an enormous skillet, cook frankfurter over medium heat 6-8 minutes or until not, at this point pink, breaking into disintegrates; channel. Blend oil and garlic; spread over pizza outside layers. Sprinkle each with 1/4 cup mozzarella cheddar. Top with pepperoni, arugula, cooked hotdog and remaining mozzarella cheddar; sprinkle with Parmesan cheddar.

5. Heat 10-15 minutes or until outside and cheddar are gently browned. Whenever wanted, top with extra arugula prior to serving.

Nutrition Facts

- 1 piece: 310 calories
- 17g fat (6g saturated fat)
- 34mg cholesterol
- 751mg sodium
- 25g carbohydrate (1g sugars, 1g fiber)
- 14g protein.

8. Creamy Broccoli and Bacon Soup

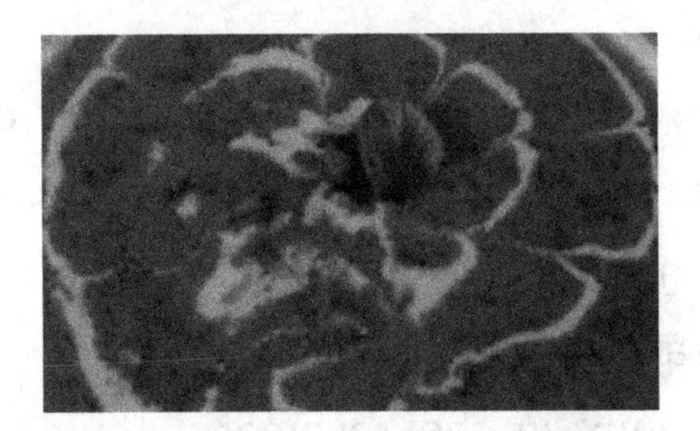

(Ready in about 20 minutes | Servings 4)

Things We Need

- Two slices bacon, chopped
- 2 tbsp. scallions, chopped
- one carrot, chopped
- one celery, chopped
- salt, and black pepper, to taste
- one teaspoon garlic, finely chopped
- ½ teaspoon dried rosemary
- one sprig thyme, stripped and chopped
- ½ head green cabbage, shredded
- ½ head broccoli, broken into florets
- 3 cups water
- one mug of chicken stock
- ½ mug full-fat yogurt

How To Start

1. Heat a stockpot; now, sear the bacon until crisp: Reserve the bacon and one tablespoon of fat.
2. Then, cook scallions, carrots, and celery in 1 tablespoon of reserved fat. Put salt, pepper, and garlic; cook an extra 1 minute or until fragrant.
3. Now, mix in the rosemary, thyme, cabbage, and broccoli. Pour in water and stock, bringing to a rapid boil; lower flame and let it simmer for 10 minutes more.
4. Put yogurt and cook an extra 5 minutes, mixing occasionally. Use an immersion blender to puree your soup until smooth.
5. Taste and adjust the seasonings. Garnish with the cooked bacon just before serving.

Each Serving:

- 233 Calories
- 15.3grams Fat
- 5.5grams Carbs
- 3.9grams Fiber
- 9.9grams Protein
- 1.3grams Sugars

9. Cauliflower Rice

(Ready in about 15 minutes | Servings 3)

Things We Need

- ½ pound cauliflower
- one tablespoon sesame oil
- ½ mug leeks, chopped
- one garlic pressed salt and
- dark pepper, to taste
- ½ teaspoon Chinese five-spice powder
- one teaspoon oyster sauce
- ½ teaspoon light soy sauce
- one tablespoon Shaoxing wine three eggs

How To Start

1. Pulse the cauliflower until it resembles rice.
2. Heat the sesame oil in a cooking pan over medium to high heat; sauté the leeks and garlic for 2 to 3 minutes. Put the prepared cauliflower rice into the cooking pan, along with salt, black pepper, and Chinese five-spice powder.
3. Next, put oyster sauce, soy sauce, and wine. Let it cook, occasionally mixing, until the cauliflower is crisp-tender, about 5 minutes.
4. Then, put the eggs into the cooking pan; mix until everything is well combined. Serve warm and enjoy!

Each Serving:

- 344 Calories
- 25.1grams Fat
- 5.7grams Carbs
- 3.4grams Fiber
- 13grams Protein
- 0.9grams Sugars

10. Easy southern Curry

(Ready in about 1 hour | Servings 4)

Things We Need

- Three teaspoons sesame oil
- 1 pound turkey wings, boneless and chopped
- two cloves garlic, finely chopped
- one small-sized red chili pepper
- ½ teaspoon turmeric powder
- ½ teaspoon ginger powder
- one teaspoon red curry paste
- one mug of unsweetened coconut milk, preferably homemade
- ½ mug water
- ½ mug turkey consommé
- Kosher salt and black pepper, to taste

How To Start

1. Heat sesame oil in a sauté cooking pan. Put the turkey and cook until it is lightly brown, about 7 minutes.
2. Put garlic, chili pepper, turmeric powder, ginger powder, and curry paste and cook for 3 minutes longer.
3. Put the milk, water, and consommé. Garnish with salt and black pepper—Cook for 45 minutes. Enjoy your meal!

Each Serving:

- 255 Calories
- 18.5grams Fat
- 4.9grams Carbs
- 4grams Fiber
- 13grams Protein
- 0.9grams Sugars

11. Ranch Chicken Breasts with Cheese

(Ready in about 20 minutes | Servings 4)

Things We Need

- Two chicken breasts
- 2 tbsp. butter, melted
- one teaspoon salt
- ½ teaspoon garlic powder
- ½ teaspoon cayenne pepper
- ½ teaspoon black peppercorns, crushed
- ½ tablespoon ranch seasoning mix
- 4 ounces Ricotta cheese, room temperature
- ½ mug Monterey-Jack cheese, four slices bacon, chopped
- ¼ mug scallions, chopped

How To Start

1. Start preparing it by preheating your oven to 370 degrees F.
2. Drizzle the chicken with melted butter. Rub the chicken with salt, garlic powder, cayenne pepper, black pepper, and ranch seasoning mix.
3. Heat a cast-iron skillet—Cook, the chicken for 3 to 5 minutes per side. Transfer all the chicken to a lightly greased baking dish.
4. Put cheese and bacon—Bake for about 12 minutes. Top with scallions just before serving. Enjoy your meal!

Each Serving:

- 290 Calories
- 18.5grams Fat
- 6.4grams Carbs
- 4.2grams Fiber
- 13grams Protein

12. Keto Southern Chicken Drumsticks

(Ready in about 20 minutes | Servings 2)

Things We Need

- One tablespoon peanut oil
- two chicken drumsticks
- ½ mug vegetable broth
- ½ mug cream cheese
- 2 cups baby spinach
- Salt and dark pepper, to taste
- ½ teaspoon parsley flakes
- ½ teaspoon shallot powder
- ½ teaspoon garlic powder
- ½ mug Asiago cheese

Direction:

1. Combine almond milk, lemon juice, 2 tablespoons of salt, 1 teaspoon of pepper and 1 teaspoon of dried oregano in a bowl.
2. Submerge chicken pieces and leave to brine for a minimum of 90 minutes and a maximum of overnight.
3. Once brining is complete, add remaining ingredients, except cooking oil, into a food processor and pulse until combined into fine crumbs.
4. Preheat oven to 180 °C/ 355 °F (fan assisted), or 200 °C/ 400 °F (conventional). Shake crumbed coating out onto a tray. One at a time, remove chicken pieces from brine solution and roll in coating until evenly coated.
5. Place coated pieces on a lined baking tray. Once all pieces are coated, bake for approx. 45 minutes depending on the size of your pieces. Mid-way through the baking time, remove from oven and spray with olive oil cooking spray.
6. Serve with Keto French Fries!

13. Hoisin Sriracha southern Chicken

Total Time: 1 hr. |Prep: 20 min |Bake: 40 min. |Makes: 4 servings

Ingredients

1/3 cup hoisin sauce
1/3 cup diminished sodium soy sauce
2 tablespoons maple syrup
2 tablespoons Sriracha bean stew sauce
1 tablespoon rice vinegar
2 teaspoons sesame oil
2 garlic cloves, minced
1/2 teaspoon minced new gingerroot
4 bone-in chicken thighs (6 ounces each)
1/4 teaspoon salt
1/4 teaspoon pepper
1 medium yam, cut into 3/4-inch 3D shapes
2 tablespoons olive oil, partitioned
4 cups new cauliflowerets
1 medium sweet red pepper, cut into 3/4-inch pieces
Sesame seeds, optional

Directions

1. Preheat oven to 400°. Whisk together the initial 8 ingredients. Put in a safe spot.
2. Sprinkle the two sides of chicken with salt and pepper. Spot chicken and yam in a solitary layer in a foil-lined 15x10x1-in. preparing dish. Sprinkle with 1 tablespoon olive oil and 33% of the hoisin blend; throw to cover.
3. Prepare 15 minutes; turn chicken and potatoes. Add cauliflower and red pepper; shower with another third of the hoisin combination and staying olive oil. Prepare until a thermometer embedded in chicken peruses 170°-175°, around 25 minutes longer. Shower with the excess hoisin combination. Whenever wanted, sprinkle with sesame seeds.

Nutrition Facts

- 1 serving:
- 490 calories
- 24g fat (5g saturated fat)
- 81mg cholesterol
- 1665mg sodium
- 40g carbohydrate (23g sugars, 5g fiber)
- 28g protein.

14. Mini Meat Loaf Sheet-Pan Meal (Keto southern recipe)

Total Time: 1hr 15 min |Prep: 35 min. Bake: 40 min |Makes: 6 servings

Ingredients

- 2 huge eggs, delicately beaten
- 1 cup tomato juice
- 3/4 cup speedy cooking oats
- 1/4 cup finely chopped onion
- 1/2 teaspoon salt
- 1-1/2 pounds lean ground meat (90% lean)
- 1/4 cup ketchup
- 3 tablespoons brown sugar
- 1 teaspoon arranged mustard
- 1/4 teaspoon ground nutmeg
- 3 huge potatoes, stripped and cut into 1/2-inch pieces
- 3 tablespoons olive oil, separated
- 1/2 teaspoon garlic salt, separated

- 1/4 teaspoon pepper, separated
- 1 pound new asparagus, managed and split

Directions

1. Preheat oven to 425°. In a huge bowl, consolidate eggs, tomato juice, oats, onion and salt. Add meat; blend daintily however completely. Shape into six 4x2-1/2-in. portions; place on a sheet dish or huge shallow cooking skillet. Join ketchup, brown sugar, mustard and nutmeg; brush over portions.
2. Consolidate potatoes with 2 tablespoons oil, 1/4 teaspoon garlic salt and 1/8 teaspoon pepper; throw to cover. Add to dish in a solitary layer. Prepare 25 minutes.
3. Consolidate asparagus with staying 1 tablespoon oil, 1/4 teaspoon garlic salt and 1/8 teaspoon pepper; throw to cover. Add to dish. Prepare until a thermometer embedded into meat portions peruses 160° and vegetables are delicate, 15-20 minutes. Let stand 5-10 minutes prior to serving.

Nutrition Facts

- 1 meat loaf with 1-1/4 cups vegetables:
- 460 calories
- 19g fat (5g saturated fat)
- 133mg cholesterol
- 690mg sodium
- 45g carbohydrate (13g sugars, 3g fiber)
- 29g protein.

15. Roasted Kabocha Squash

Prep Time: 25 Minutes |Cook Time: 1 Hour | Total Time: 1 Hour 25 Minutes |Servings: 4

Ingredients

- 1 medium (around 2 lb./1 kg) kabocha squash (or oak seed squash, or butternut squash)
- 1 medium yellow onion , skin on
- inches (4 cm) ginger , generally chopped
- 6 cloves garlic
- 2 tablespoons maple syrup
- 1 tablespoon olive oil
- 1/2 teaspoons salt , separated
- 1/2 teaspoon cumin powder
- 1 cup vegetable stock
- 2 tablespoons margarine (or olive oil for a vegetarian dish)
- Dark pepper for decorate (Optional)
- Newly chopped sage or thyme for decorate (Optional)

Guidelines

1. Preheat oven to 425 °F (220 °C).
2. Cut the squash into quarters (see blog entry above to figure out how to cut kabocha securely). Cut the onion into quarters, leaving the skin on. Slash the ginger and strip the garlic cloves.
3. Line a heating plate with material paper. Spread the kabocha squash, onion, ginger and garlic on the plate.
4. Sprinkle with 1 tablespoon maple syrup, the olive oil, and the maple syrup. Rub it on to the squash equitably with your hands. Sprinkle 1/2 teaspoon of salt over it.
5. Turn the squash and onions to be skin-side-up. Ensure the garlic cloves are under the hoods of the squash to help them keep wet.
6. Cook for 1 hour at 425 °F (220 °C). Flip the squash and onions at the brief imprint, actually skin-side-up, and the other cut side down.
7. When the vegetables are done, allowed them to cool for 5 to 10 minutes on the kitchen counter, until you can deal with the squash with your hands.
8. Using a blade, strip the skin off the squash and dispose of it. Eliminate the dried layer from the onions and dispose of it.
9. Add the broiled veggies, the excess 1 tablespoon maple syrup, and the leftover 1 teaspoon salt, alongside the cumin, vegetable stock, and spread, to the blender, Blend on high until smooth, around 5 minutes. Taste the soup. Change the surface by adding more stock as wanted, and change the flavoring by

adding more salt if necessary. At that point mix again to blend well.

10. Enhancement with olive oil (or substantial cream), chopped sage or thyme, and newly ground dark pepper, if necessary. Serve hot with toasted bread. Enjoy!

Nutrition

- Serving: 1serving
- Calories: 220kcal
- Carbohydrates: 30.8g
- Protein: 4.7g, Fat: 9.8g
- Saturated Fat: 4.3g
- Cholesterol: 15mg
- Sodium: 817mg
- Potassium: 155mg
- Fiber: 3.6g
- Sugar: 15.4g
- Calcium: 83mg
- Iron: 2mg

16. Southern Shrimp Soup

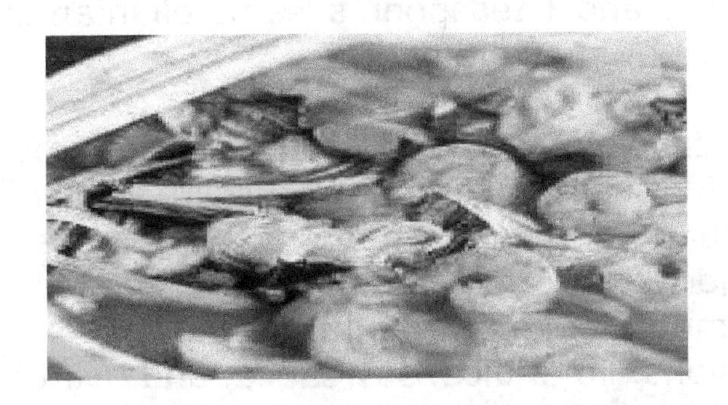

Prep: 15 min |Cook: 17 min |Total: 32 min |Yield: Makes: 4

Ingredients:
3 ounces thin rice noodles
2 teaspoons sesame oil, divided
2 teaspoons canola oil
4 ounces sliced shitake mushroom
4 cups (32 ounces) boxed low-sodium vegetable broth
2 cups grated carrots (about 1)
1 (1-inch) piece ginger, peeled and cut into 4 (1/4-inch) coins
1/2 pound medium shrimp, peeled and deveined (about 20 shrimp)
2 cups sliced scallions
2 teaspoons fresh lime juice
1 1/2 teaspoons low-sodium soy sauce
2 tablespoons chopped fresh cilantro
2 tablespoons fresh mint leaves
Directions
Step 1

Heat an enormous pot of water to the point of boiling; eliminate skillet from heat. Add noodles; let splash just until delicate (around 8 minutes). Channel the noodles in a colander; flush. Throw the noodles and 1 teaspoon sesame oil in an enormous bowl; put in a safe spot.
Step 2
Add canola oil to skillet; sauté mushrooms over medium heat, mixing until delicate and brilliant (around 2–3 minutes). Add stock, carrots, and ginger; stew 5 minutes. Add shrimp; stew until shrimp is cooked through (around 2 minutes). Mix in scallions, lime juice, soy sauce, and half of spices.
Step 3
Split noodles between 4 serving bowls; spoon soup over noodles. Sprinkle soup with outstanding spices; shower each with the leftover sesame oil.
Nutrition Facts

- Per Serving:
- 203 calories
- Fat 5g
- Saturated fat 1g
- Mono fat 2g
- Poly fat 2g
- Cholesterol 84mg
- Protein 10g
- Carbohydrates 29g
- Sugars 3g
- Fiber 2g
- Iron 2mg
- Sodium 518mg
- Calcium 39mg.

17. Coriander-&-Lemon-Crusted Salmon with Asparagus Salad & Poached Egg

Total: 45 min | Servings: 4

Ingredients

- 1 tablespoon coriander seeds
- 1 teaspoon lemon zing
- ¾ teaspoon fine ocean salt, separated
- ½ teaspoon squashed red pepper
- 1 pound wild salmon , skin-on, cut into 4 parts
- 1 pound asparagus, managed
- 2 tablespoons extra-virgin olive oil
- 1 tablespoon lemon juice
- 1 tablespoon chopped new mint
- 1 tablespoon chopped new tarragon
- ¼ teaspoon ground pepper, in addition to additional for embellish
- 8 cups water
- 1 tablespoon white vinegar
- 4 huge eggs

Directions:

Stage 1

1. Position a rack in upper third of oven; preheat grill to high. Coat a rimmed preparing sheet with cooking splash.

Stage 2

1. Toast coriander in a little skillet over medium heat, shaking the pan much of the time, until fragrant, around 3 minutes. Heartbeat the coriander, lemon zing, 1/2 teaspoon salt and squashed red pepper in a zest processor until finely ground. Coat the salmon substance with the flavor combination (around 1/2 teaspoons for each bit) and spot the salmon on the readied preparing sheet.

Stage 3

1. Cut off asparagus tips and daintily cut stalks on the inclining. Throw the tips and cuts with oil, lemon juice, mint, tarragon, pepper and the remaining 1/4 teaspoon salt. Let stand while you cook the salmon and eggs.

Stage 4

1. Heat water and vinegar to the point of boiling in a huge saucepan.
2. Stage 5
3. In the interim, sear the salmon until just cooked through, 3 to 6 minutes, contingent upon thickness. Tent with foil to keep warm.

Stage 6

1. Decrease the bubbling water to an exposed stew. Delicately mix in a circle so the water is whirling around the pot. Break eggs, each in turn, into the water. Cook until the whites are set yet the yolks are as yet runny, 3 to 4 minutes.

Stage 7

1. To serve, partition the asparagus serving of mixed greens and salmon among 4 plates. Make a home in every serving of mixed greens and top with a poached egg.

Nutrition Facts

- Serving Size: 3 Oz. Salmon
- 1/2 Cup Salad & 1 Egg Per Serving:
- 288 calories;
- Protein 30.5g;
- Carbohydrates 4.2g;
- Dietary fiber 1.9g;
- Sugars 1g;
- Fat 16.3g;
- Saturated fat 3.6g;
- Cholesterol 239mg;
- Vitamin a iu 1157.2IU;
- Vitamin c 8.4mg;
- Folate 121.9mcg;
- Calcium 115.3mg;
- Iron 2.4mg;
- Magnesium 57.4mg;
- Potassium 658.8mg;
- Sodium 360.1mg;
- Thiamin 0.2mg.

- Exchanges:
- 1/2 Vegetable,
- 4 Lean Meat,
- 1 1/2 Fat

18. Southern Keto burger Skillet with Bacon and Mushrooms

(Ready in about 20 minutes | Servings 4)

Things We Need

- Two slices of Canadian bacon
- Chopped ½ mug shallots
- sliced one garlic clove
- 1 pound pork salt, and dark pepper, to taste
- 1/3 mug vegetable broth
- ¼ mug white wine
- 6 ounces Cremini mushrooms
- sliced ½ mug cream cheese

How To Start

1. Heat a cast-iron skillet. Cook the bacon for almost 2 to 3 minutes; reserve the bacon and one tablespoon of fat. Then, sauté the shallots and garlic in 1 tablespoon of bacon fat until tender and fragrant.
2. Put the pork, salt, and black pepper into the skillet. Cook for 4 to 5 minutes or until the meat is nicely browned.
3. Put broth, wine, and mushrooms—cover and cook for 8 to 9 minutes over medium flame.
4. Turn off the heat. Put cream cheese and mix to combine. Serve topped with the reserved bacon. Enjoy!

Each Serving:

- 401 Calories
- 25.1grams Fat
- 4.9grams Carbs
- 4.2grams Fiber
- 11.3grams Protein
- 0.7grams Sugars

19. Southern Country-Style Pork Stew

(Ready in about 40 minutes | Servings 4)

Things We Need

- 2 tbsp. lard, room temperature
- ¼ mug leeks, chopped
- two garlic cloves,
- 1 (1-inch) piece ginger root, chopped
- one bell pepper, seeded and chopped
- 1 pound pork stew meat, cubed
- ½ mug tomato paste
- 2 cups chicken broth
- salt & black pepper, to taste
- one teaspoon paprika
- one bay leaf
- ¼ mug Crème fraiche

How To Start

1. Melt the lard in a sauté cooking pan that is preheated. Then, cook the leeks, garlic, and ginger until aromatic, about 3 minutes.
2. Put bell pepper and cook for a further 2 minutes, mixing periodically. Put the pork and cook for an extra 3 minutes or until no longer pink.
3. Mix in the tomato paste, broth, salt, pepper, paprika, and bay leaf. Cover and let it simmer over low-medium heat for 30 minutes.
4. Mix in Crème fraiche; turn off the heat and mix until everything is well combined. Spoon into serving casseroles and serve immediately.

Each Serving:

- 255 Calories
- 15.3grams Fat
- 6grams Carbs
- 3.4grams Fiber
- 10.9grams Protein
- 0.9grams Sugar

20. Buttery Pork Chops

(Ready in about 20 minutes | Servings 2)

Things We Need

- ½ stick butter with room temperature
- ½ mug white onion, chopped
- 4 ounces button mushrooms, sliced
- 1/3 pound pork loin chops
- one teaspoon dried parsley flakes
- Salt & black pepper, to taste
- ½ mug Swiss cheese, shredded

How To Start

1. Melt ¼ of the butter stick in a skillet. Then, sauté the onions and mushrooms until the onions are translucent and the mushrooms are tender and fragrant for about 5 minutes. Reserve.
2. Then, melt the remaining ¼ of the butter stick and cook pork until slightly browned on all sides, about 10 minutes.
3. Put the onion batter, parsley, salt, and pepper. Lastly, top with cheese; cover and let it cook on medium-low flame until cheese has melted.
4. Serve immediately and enjoy!

Each Serving:

- 255 Calories
- 20.0grams Fat
- 4.9grams Carbs
- 4.2grams Fiber
- 9.9grams Protein
- 1.9grams Sugars

21. Hazelnut-Parsley Roast Tilapia

Active: 20 min | Total: 30 min | Servings: 4 (4x11)

Ingredients

- 2 tablespoons olive oil, partitioned
- 4 (5 ounce) tilapia filets (new or frozen, defrosted)
- ⅓ cup finely chopped hazelnuts
- ¼ cup finely chopped new parsley
- 1 little shallot, minced
- 2 teaspoons lemon zing
- ⅛ teaspoon salt in addition to 1/4 teaspoon, partitioned
- ¼ teaspoon ground pepper, partitioned
- 1 ½ tablespoons lemon juice

Directions:

Stage 1

1. Preheat oven to 450 degrees F. Line a huge rimmed preparing sheet with foil; brush with 1 Tbsp. oil. Carry fish to room temperature by allowing it to remain on the counter for 15 minutes.

Stage 2

2. In the meantime, mix together hazelnuts, parsley, shallot, lemon zing, 1 tsp. oil, 1/8 tsp. salt, and 1/8 tsp. pepper in a little bowl.

Stage 3

3. Wipe the two sides of the fish off with a paper towel. Spot the fish on the readied heating sheet. Brush the two sides of the fish with lemon juice and the remaining 2 tsp. oil. Season the two sides equitably with the remaining 1/4 tsp. salt and 1/8 tsp. pepper. Gap the hazelnut combination equally among the highest points of the filets and pat tenderly to follow.

Stage 4

4. Broil the fish until it is obscure, firm, and simply starting to piece, 7 to 10 minutes. Serve right away.

Nutrition Facts

- Serving Size: 4 Oz.
- Fish Per Serving: 262 calories
- protein 30.2g
- carbohydrates 3.3g
- dietary fiber 1.2g
- sugars 0.8g; fat 15g
- saturated fat 2.2g
- cholesterol 70.9mg
- vitamin a iu 378.9IU
- vitamin c 9.5mg
- folate 53.4mcg
- calcium 34.5mg
- iron 1.6mg
- magnesium 57.4mg
- potassium 539.6mg
- Sodium 294.7mg.

22. Keto Shrimp Etouffee with Crawfish

Prep Time: 5 min | Cook Time: 25 min | Total Time: 30 min

Ingredients

- 1 pound crude enormous shrimp stripped and deveined,
- 1 pound crayfish tails defrosted
- 4 Tbsp. spread
- 1 cup diced celery
- 1 cup diced ringer pepper
- ¾ cup diced onion
- 4 cloves garlic finely chopped
- 1 tsp. paprika
- 1 tsp. dried oregano
- 1 tsp. dried thyme
- ¼ tsp. cayenne pepper
- ½ tsp. pepper
- ½ tsp. salt
- 1 cup shrimp or chicken stock
- ½ cup weighty cream

- 3 oz. cream cheddar relaxed
- ¼ cup cut green onions
- Embellishment: Chopped Parsley
- Steamed Cauliflower Rice

Guidelines

1. In an enormous skillet over medium heat, add margarine. Soften spread and keep on cooking, blending once in a while, for 3-5 minutes or until the margarine is delicately browned. Add the diced celery, onion, and pepper to the spread and keep on cooking until the onion is clear and the veggies begin to brown, around 5-7 minutes.
2. In a little bowl join the paprika, oregano, thyme, peppers and salt and put in a safe spot. Add the chopped garlic to the veggies and cook one more moment.
3. Add the zest combination into the veggies and cook for one more moment, blending continually. Add the stock to the veggie and flavor blend and mix well to join. Stew uncovered for 6-8 minutes. Add the cream to the skillet and keep on stewing for another 5-7 minutes or until the combination has thickened and will cover the rear of a spoon.
4. When the sauce has thickened, add the crayfish and shrimp to the skillet. Cook 2-3 minutes until the shrimp is cooked through. Eliminate the skillet from the heat and mix in the cream cheddar until completely softened and fused.
5. Sprinkle the green onions over the highest point of the shrimp and crayfish and trimming

with chopped parsley whenever wanted. Serve over steamed cauliflower rice.

Notes

1. To thicken the sauce with the assistance of Xanthum gum rather than the cream cheddar, add around 1/8 tsp. at a time until you arrive at your ideal consistency.

Nutrition

- Calories: 427kcal
- Carbohydrates: 8g
- Protein: 24g
- Fat: 32g
- Sodium: 1318mg
- Potassium: 447mg
- Fiber: 3g
- Sugar: 4g
- Calcium: 252mg
- Iron: 4mg

23. Saucy Skirt Steak with Broccoli

(Ready in about 15 minutes| Servings 3)

Things We Need

- ½ pound skirt steak, sliced into pieces
- 2 tbsp. butter, room temperature
- ½ pound broccoli
- ½ mug scallions
- Chopped one clove garlic, pressed Marinade
- ½ teaspoon black pepper
- One teaspoon red pepper flakes
- ½ teaspoon salt
- 2 tbsp. olive oil
- One tablespoon tamari sauce

- ¼ mug wine vinegar

How To Start

1. In a ceramic casserole, thoroughly combine all components for the marinade. Put the beef and allow it to sit in your refrigerator for 2 hours.
2. Melt one tablespoon of butter in a skillet over high to medium to high heat. Cook the broccoli for 2 minutes, frequently mixing, until it is tender but bright green. Reserve.
3. Melt the remaining butter in the skillet. Once hot, cook the scallions and garlic until aromatic, about 2 minutes. Reserve.
4. Next, sear the beef, adding a small amount of the marinade. Cook until these are well browned on all sides or about 10 minutes.
5. Put the reserved vegetables and cook for a few minutes more or until everything is heated through. Enjoy your meal!

Nutritional Value:

Each Serving:

- 233 Calories
- 25.1grams Fat
- 6grams Carbs
- 4grams Fiber
- 12.2grams Protein

24. Classic southern Beef Stroganoff

(Ready in about 1 hour | Servings 4)

Things We Need

- 2 tbsp. lard, room temperature
- 1 pound beef stew meat, cut across the grain into strips
- ½ yellow onion, peeled and chopped two garlic cloves
- 4 ounces mushrooms, sliced
- ½ teaspoon salt one teaspoon smoked paprika
- ¼ teaspoon black pepper
- ½ teaspoon dried basil
- ¼ mug red cooking wine
- 4 cups vegetable broth one tomato, pureed two celery stalks, chopped

- ½ mug sour cream

How To Start

1. Melt the lard in a stockpot. Then, cook the meat until nicely browned on all sides.
2. Then, put onion and garlic and cook until they are fragrant. Now, mix in the mushrooms and cook until they are tender.
3. Put seasonings, wine, broth, tomato, and celery. Lower heat, cover it and simmer for 50 minutes.
4. Turn off the flame and put sour cream; mix until heated through. Taste, adjust the seasonings and serve warm. Enjoy your meal!

Each Serving:

- 344 Calories
- 25.1grams Fat
- 6.4grams Carbs
- 4.2grams Fiber
- 9.9grams Protein
- 0.9grams Sugars

25. Keto southern Catfish and Cauliflower Casserole

(Ready in about 30 minutes | Servings 4)

Things We Need

- One tablespoon sesame oil
- 11 ounces cauliflower
- Four scallions
- One garlic clove,
- One teaspoon ginger root, salt, and black pepper, to taste Cayenne pepper, to taste
- Two sprigs dried thyme, crushed
- One sprig of crushed rosemary,
- take 24 ounces catfish, cut into pieces ½ mug cream cheese

- ½ double mug cream
- One egg
- 2 ounces butter

How To Start

1. Start by giving a preheat to your oven to 390 degrees F. Now, lightly grease a casserole dish with a nonstick cooking spray.
2. Then, heat the oil in a cooking pan over medium to high heat; once it becomes hot; cook the scallions and cauliflower until tender or 5 to 6 minutes. Put the garlic and ginger; in that and continue for one more minute to sauté.
3. Transfer all the vegetables to the prepared casserole dish. Sprinkle with seasonings. Put catfish to the top.
4. In a mixing casserole, thoroughly combine the cream cheese, double cream, and egg. Spread this creamy butter on the top of the casserole.
5. Top with slices of the butter and then bake in the preheated oven for about 18 to 22 minutes or until the fish can be flaked easily with a fork. Enjoy your meal!

Each Serving:

- 518 Calories
- 20.0grams Fat
- 5.5grams Carbs
- 3.9grams Fiber
- 10.9grams Protein
- 1.3grams Sugars

26. Southern Herring Salad

(Ready in about 10 minutes | Servings 3)

Things We Need

- 6 ounces of pickled herring pieces, drained and flaked
- ½ mug baby spinach
- 2 tbsp. basil leaves
- 2 tbsp. chives, chopped one teaspoon garlic,
- One bell pepper, chopped
- One red onion, chopped
- 2 tbsp. key lime juice,
- Squeezed salt and black pepper to taste

How To Start

1. In a salad casserole, combine the herring pieces with spinach, chives, basil leaves, garlic, red onion, and bell pepper.
2. Then, drizzle the key lime juice over the salad; put salt and pepper to taste and toss to combine. Smalling måltid! Enjoy your meal!

Each Serving:

- 411 Calories
- 18.5grams Fat
- 4.9grams Carbs
- 3.9grams Fiber
- 12.2grams Protein
- 0.9grams Sugars

27. Southern Fruity Mini Pancake Skewers

Prep Time: 20-mins |Cooking Time: 10-mins|Servings: 10

Ingredients

Pancakes:

- 1 cup all-purpose flour
- 2 tablespoons white sugar
- 2 teaspoons baking powder
- ¼ teaspoon baking soda
- ¼ teaspoon ground cinnamon
- ¼ teaspoon salt
- ¾ cup milk
- 1 large egg

- 1 tablespoon melted unsalted butter
- 1 teaspoon amaretto extract
- Skewers:
- 1 pint strawberries, sliced horizontally
- 1/4 cup blueberry cream cheese spread (such as Philadelphia®)
- 1 medium banana, sliced
- 1 tablespoon confectioners' sugar, or to taste
- 10 bamboo skewers, or as needed

Directions

1. Whisk together flour, sugar, baking powder, baking soda, cinnamon, and salt in a bowl. Whisk milk, egg, butter, and amaretto extract together in a second bowl. Pour wet ingredients into the flour mixture, and mix until batter is well combined and smooth.

2. Heat a large nonstick skillet or griddle over medium heat. Drop teaspoonful of batter onto the hot skillet to form 1-inch diameter pancakes. Cook for about 1 to 2 minutes, flip, and continue cooking until golden brown, about 1 more minute. Transfer cooked pancakes to a plate and repeat with remaining batter.

3. Stack ingredients on a work surface as follows: pancake, banana, pancake spread with cream cheese, pancake, strawberry, and pancake. (Each skewer will use 4 pancakes.) Insert a skewer through the center of the stack and repeat to make remaining skewers.
4. Dust with confectioner's sugar, and serve.

Nutrition Facts

- Per Serving: 97 calories
- protein 2.7g
- carbohydrates 16.8g
- fat 2.2g
- cholesterol 23.1mg
- sodium 202.2mg

28. Southern burger breakfast

Prep Time: 10-mins|Cooking Time: 5-mins|Servings: 1 burger

Ingredients

- 1 breakfast sausage patty or 2 slices of bacon
- 1 egg
- 1 slice American cheese
- 1 hamburger bun

Instructions

1. Place a skillet over medium heat and cook the sausage or bacon in the skillet.
2. Once the sausage or bacon has started to release some of the grease, place a wide mouth canning ring onto the skillet.
3. Crack one egg and place the egg inside of the canning ring.
4. Continue to cook the sausage or bacon and remove it from the skillet when done, draining on paper towels.
5. Flip the egg over and allow the other side to cook. The sandwiches are served with solid, not runny yolks. When the egg has finished cooking (it should take about 30 seconds once you have flipped it over), remove it from the pan.
6. To assemble the sandwich, place the sausage or bacon on the bottom bun. You can break the bacon in half so it will fit the hamburger bun.
7. Add the egg, and then top with cheese. Place the top bun on top of the cheese.

Nutrition Information

- Calories: 442kcal
- Carbohydrates: 22g
- Protein: 22g
- Fat: 28g
- Saturated Fat: 10g
- Cholesterol: 227mg
- Sodium: 1009mg
- Potassium: 264mg
- Fiber: 0g
- Sugar: 3g
- Vitamin A: 435IU
- Calcium: 319mg
- Iron: 2.9mg

29. Southern Pecan Cake Bars

Prep Time: 10 min |Cook Time: 30 min |Total Time: 40 min | Servings: 12 Calories: 353kcal

Ingredients

- 1 cup sugar
- 1 cup brown sugar
- 4 eggs
- 1 cup vegetable oil
- 1 ½ cups self-rising flour
- 1 tsp. vanilla
- 2 cups chopped pecans

Guidelines

1. Preheat oven to 350F degrees. Shower the base just of a 9x13 glass preparing dish with nonstick cooking splash.
2. In a medium bowl, combine as one sugar, brown sugar, eggs and oil until smooth. Tenderly mix in flour and vanilla. At long last, blend in 1 ½ cups chopped walnut.
3. Fill arranged heating dish.
4. Sprinkle top uniformly with remaining (½ cup) chopped walnuts
5. Heat for 40-50 minutes until an inserted toothpick in the center tells the truth. Oven times may shift (If it begins to get excessively brown on top, cover with aluminum foil until it is done preparing.)

Notes

1. You can utilize whatever nut you like in this. Walnuts and pecans work the best in this.
2. You could likewise make a shower sauce for it in the event that you'd like. I have a very straightforward formula for it over on my Southern Pecan Praline Cake. It's a particularly flexible sauce and is totally flawlessness over frozen yogurt as well or attempt Salted Caramel.
3. Try not to make them rise flour? You can make it! For some flour, whisk along with 1 ½ teaspoons of heating powder and ¼ teaspoon of salt. Make a point to whisk these ingredients together well so the heating powder and salt are both equally circulated inside the flour.

4. Take a stab at adding cinnamon chips or chocolate chips to this. It truly switches up the flavor!

Nutrition

- Calories: 353kcal
- Carbohydrates: 48g
- Protein: 5g
- Fat: 16g
- Saturated Fat: 3g
- Cholesterol: 54mg
- Sodium: 26mg
- Potassium: 134mg
- Fiber: 2g
- Sugar: 35g
- Vitamin A: 90IU
- Vitamin C: 0.2mg
- Calcium: 38mg
- Iron: 1mg

30. Southern Tea Cakes

Prep Time: 5 min | Cook Time: 10 min | Total Time: 15 min | Servings: 12 servings | Calories: 180kcal

Ingredients

- 1 stick unsalted spread room temperature
- 3/4 cup granulated sugar
- 1 huge egg at room temperature
- 2 teaspoons unadulterated vanilla concentrate
- 1/2 cup universally handy flour
- 1/4 teaspoon salt
- 1/4 teaspoon preparing pop

Guidelines

1. In a medium measured bowl, whisk together the flour, salt and heating pop and put in a safe spot.
2. In the bowl of your blender, gather spread and sugar and blend into a single unit on high velocity until soft and smooth (around 4-5 minutes).
3. Go blender to medium speed and include one egg and vanilla concentrate and beat until all around fused.

4. In conclusion, go blender to moderate speed and include flour combination in time periods beating after every expansion to fuse.
5. After batter is very much blended, turn off blender and eliminate mixture from blender and add to a Ziploc pack and spot in your cooler for in any event one hour to solidify batter.
6. When mixture is firm, eliminate from ice chest and preheat your oven to 325 degrees.
7. Line your treat sheet with material paper.
8. Taking an estimating tablespoon, scoop out treat batter the size of the tablespoon and fold into a ball. Using your thumb, delicately press the middle to smooth a piece and spot on the plate.
9. Do likewise for the remainder of the mixture leaving in any event a 1/2 crawl between every batter ball.
10. Heat for 9-11 minutes until brilliant brown on the edges and eliminate from the oven.
11. Cool for 5-10 minutes and serve.

Notes

- Make sure to ensure your ingredients are room temperature. They will consolidate much better and make an awesome all around blended mixture.

Nutrition

- Calories: 180kcal
- Carbohydrates: 24g
- Protein: 2g
- Fat: 8g
- Saturated Fat: 4g
- Cholesterol: 35mg
- Sodium: 78mg
- Potassium: 22mg
- Sugar: 12g
- Vitamin A: 260IU
- Calcium: 7mg
- Iron: 0.8mg

31. Southern Keto Fettuccine

Ingredients

- 1-2 pounds dry spinach fettuccine (or 2 pounds fresh)
- 1/2 cup chopped cilantro (2 tablespoons for garnish/finishing)
- 2-tablespoons of chopped fresh garlic
- 2-tablespoons chopped jalapeno pepper (seeds and veins can be removed if a milder flavor is desired)
- 3-tablespoons unsalted butter (reserve tablespoons per container)
- 1/2 cup of chicken stock
- 2-tablespoons of tequila
- 2-tablespoons of freshly squeezed lime juice
- 3-tablespoons of soy sauce
- 1/2 pound chicken breast diced 3/4 inch

- 1/4 cup red onion thinly sliced
- 1 1/2 cup of red bell pepper thinly sliced
- 1/2 cup of yellow bell pepper thinly sliced
- 1/2 cup green pepper thinly sliced
- 1 1/2 cups of cream

Directions

1. Quickly prepare to boil salted water for cooking pasta; cook dinner al dente, for dry pasta for 8 to 10 minutes, for bubbly for about three minutes. Pasta can be cooked, rinsed, and oiled slightly ahead of time, after which it is "flashed" in boiling water or cooked to match the sauce/topping.
2. Mix 1/3 cup of cilantro, garlic, and jalapeno over medium heat in 2 tablespoons of oil for four to 5 minutes. Remove lime juice, tequila, and stock. Bring the combination to a boil and cook to a pasty consistency until reduced; put aside.
3. Pour over the diced soy sauce; Set aside for 5 minutes. Meanwhile, prepare evening onions and peppers with the last of butter over medium heat, stirring occasionally. Toss and add the reserved vegetables and cream when the vegetable wilt (go limp), add the chook and soy sauce.
4. Bring the sauce to a boil; cook gently until the chicken has melted and the sauce is thick (about 3 minutes).

Nutritional Value

- Calories: 1077 kcal
- Carbohydrates: 91 g
- Protein: 57 g
- Fat: 51 g
- Saturated fat: 1057 mg
- Potassium: 1204 mg
- Fiber: 5 g
- Sugar: 5 g
- Vitamin A: 2600 IE
- Vitamin C: 89.2 mg
- Calcium : 119 mg
- Iron: 3.5

32. Tomato-Basil Bisque

Prep Time: 20-mins|Cooking Time: 5-mins|Servings: 5

Ingredients

- 6 celery ribs, chopped
- 1 large onion
- 1 medium sweet red pepper, chopped
- 1/4 cup butter, cubed
- 3 cans (14-1/2 ounces each) diced tomatoes, undrained
- 1 tablespoon tomato paste
- 3/4 cup loosely basil leaves, coarsely chopped
- 3 teaspoons sugar
- 2 teaspoons salt
- 1/2 teaspoon pepper

- 1-1/2 cups heavy whipping cream

Directions

1. In a large saucepan, sauté the celery, onion and red pepper in butter for 5-6 minutes or until tender. Add tomatoes and its paste. Bring to a boil. Reduce heat; cover and simmer for 40 minutes.
2. Remove from the heat. Stir in the basil, sugar, salt and pepper; cool slightly. Transfer half of the soup mixture to a blender. While processing, add cream; process until pureed. Return to the pan; heat through (do not boil).

Nutrition Facts

- 1-1/3 cups: 383 calories
- 36g fat (22g saturated fat)
- 122mg cholesterol
- 1214mg sodium
- 15g carbohydrate (10g sugars, 4g fiber)
- 3g protein.

33. Keto Southern Sweet Potato Soufflé

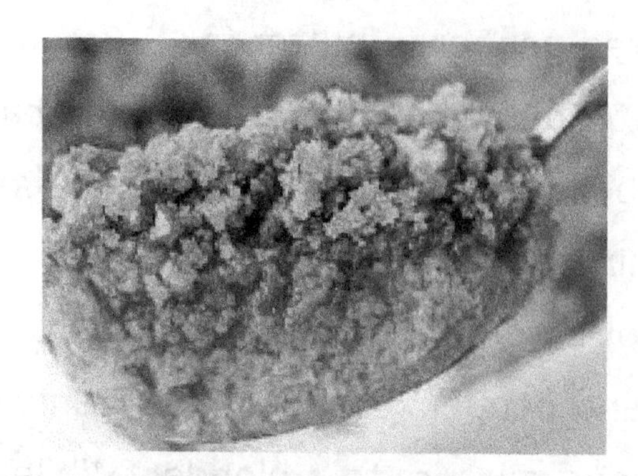

Serves: 8 servings | Prep time: 30 minutes | Cook time: 1 hour | Total time: 1 hr. 30 min

Ingredients

- 3-4 pounds yams (stripped and cubed)
- 1 stick (1/2 cup) unsalted spread (liquefied + 3 tablespoons)
- 3 huge eggs (daintily beaten)
- 1/2 cup light brown sugar
- 1 cup cream (or entire milk)
- 1/2 cup self-rising flour (or better self-rising cake flour)
- 1 teaspoon vanilla concentrate
- 1/2 teaspoon salt

- 1 cup chopped walnuts (broiled)
- Cinnamon Sugar:
- 1/4 cup white sugar (or light brown sugar)
- 1/2 teaspoon ground cinnamon
- 1/4 cup unsalted spread (liquefied)

Directions

1. Preheat oven to 350 degrees F. Orchestrate the oven rack in the oven.
2. Margarine or splash with heating shower a 9x13 inch meal or preparing dish. Put in a safe spot.
3. Add 1 cup of walnuts to a heating sheet and dish for a couple of moments. Watch near not consume them. Eliminate from oven, cool and generally cleave.

Cook Sweet Potatoes:

1. Meanwhile, add the cubed potatoes to a Dutch oven or enormous sauce dish. Cover with water and sprinkle some salt, heat to the point of boiling. Bubble for around 15 minutes, when punctured with a fork, the potatoes ought to be delicate.
2. Channel cooked yams, pound until smooth and put to the side to chill a piece.

Cinnamon Sugar:

1. Consolidate the sugar and cinnamon in a little bowl. Mix and put in a safe spot.

Plan Soufflé:

1. In a medium bowl consolidate: liquefied spread, brown sugar, beaten eggs, cream, vanilla, salt and flour. Whisk well to join; a hand blender can be utilized also.
2. Add the combination to the crushed yams and mix until very much consolidated. A hand blender can be utilized for this too.
3. Move the combination to the readied heating dish. Smooth the top.
4. Sprinkle with chopped walnuts and cinnamon sugar uniformly. Shower the excess 3 tablespoons of dissolved margarine on top.

Heat:

1. Cover dish with foil, to maintain a strategic distance from walnut beating from consuming. Heat for around 30 minutes, reveal and prepare for another 20-30 minutes or until puffed and delicately browned on the edges and top.
2. Serve quickly or cool and refrigerate for some other time.

Nutrition information

- Calories: 550
- Carbohydrates: 56
- Protein: 7
- Fat: 34
- Saturated Fat: 15
- Cholesterol: 132
- Sodium: 279
- Potassium: 700
- Fiber: 6
- Sugar: 21
- Vitamin A: 25020
- Vitamin C: 4.4
- Calcium: 104
- Iron: 1.8

34. Vegan Southern Soul Bowl

Prep: 10 min |Cook: 20 min |Total: 30 min | Servings: 4 people

Ingredients

Cornbread:

- Cornbread formula here, prep early for ease

Collards:

- 1 tbsp. olive oil, additional virgin
- 4 cups collard greens, chopped - around one pack
- 2 cloves garlic, chopped
- 1-2 tbsp. apple juice vinegar
- salt and pepper to taste

Bar-b-que Tofu:

- 10 oz. tofu, firm - cubed
- 1 cup veggie lover grill sauce, DIY or packaged

Messy Sauce:

- 3/4 cup yam, prepared - crushed - skin eliminated — 1 little potato
- 4-5 Tbsp. veggie lover spread
- 1-2 cloves garlic
- 1/3 cup healthful yeast

- 1/2 cup pasta water, + add more to mix if necessary
- 1 Tbsp. Dijon mustard
- 1/4 tsp. salt
- 1/8 tsp. turmeric, for shading – discretionary
- 1/4 cup veggie lover cheddar shreds, discretionary

Other:

- 3 cups pasta shells

Directions

Cornbread

1. For ease, I instruct making the cornbread ahead concerning time if conceivable. This way you can simply get and cut. You can utilize a simple veggie lover blend, or follow the formula connected in notes.

Bar-b-que Tofu

1. Preheat oven to 375 and fix a heating sheet with material paper.
2. In a huge blending bowl, throw the tofu blocks with the bar-b-que sauce. At that point move the shapes and sauce to the preparing sheet. Spread in a far layer, so the shapes don't cover or cover one another.
3. Prepare at 375 for 15-20 minutes. Mood killer heat and let tofu rest for a couple of moments prior to serving.

Messy Shells

1. Heat an enormous pot of water to the point of boiling and add pasta shells. Cook until delicate – make sauce while bubbling.
2. Microwave your yam for 5-7 minutes, or until delicate. Eliminate skin. Crush and measure out around 3/4 cups. You can serve any extra as another side dish.
3. Add all the messy sauce ingredients to a blender and mix from low to high until smooth.
4. Channel pasta and pour the greater part of the messy sauce up and over the pasta. Mix to consolidate and cushion. Put to the side in a warm pot with a top on.

Collards

1. You can begin your collards while your pasta is bubbling – since they just require a couple of moments. Add your olive oil and garlic to a skillet over high heat. At the point when oil is hot, include the collards. Throw a piece with the oil and garlic. At that point turn off heat and cover the collards with a top – even a weighty top will work. Allow them to sit for five minutes, at that point add the juice vinegar and salt and pepper – throw to consolidate – they ought to be pleasantly shriveled now.
2. Amass Plate
3. Add the tofu, collards, messy pasta and cornbread to each plate and serve!
4. Gear
5. Huge soup pot
6. Blender
7. Skillet
8. Preparing sheet

9. Blending bowl
10. Cornbread dish

Nutrition estimate

- per serving
- Calories: 627kcal
- Carbohydrates: 96g
- Protein: 20g
- Fat: 18g
- Saturated Fat: 3g
- Sodium: 1042mg
- Potassium: 567mg
- Fiber: 7g
- Sugar: 27g
- Vitamin A: 6040IU
- Vitamin C: 14mg
- Calcium: 222mg
- Iron: 3mg

Conclusion

I would like to thank you all for going through all the recipes. These recipes are traditional southern Keto diet recipes which are very easy and more delicious to eat. Also, you do not need to spend hours in kitchen to prepare these meals. Try these at home and appreciate.